First steps fishing

a beginners guide

By

Richard Blackburn

Copyright © 2016 Richard Blackburn

All rights reserved.

ISBN-13:
978-1523443574

Table of Contents

Introduction 6

Where to fish 7

Fishing Styles 12

Fishing Tackle 14

General purpose reel 18

Bait 32

Casting 36

Your first fishing trip 41

Basic float rigs 44

Setting up your tackle 51

Ledgering 72

Set up for feeder fishing 80

Playing fish 86

Fishing on the surface 93

Handling the fish 102

Introduction

With all the hustle and bustle of day to day life, and all the electronic gadgets these days. Fishing is a sport that can take you to quiet picturesque waterways and help you leave the modern world behind for a few hours. It is a sport for young and old and it is fun and affordable too.

Within these pages are tips and advice to start you journey into the world of fishing.

Have fun!

Where to fish

Day ticket waters

Day ticket or commercial waters have become very popular and are a good way to try fishing for the first time or return to fishing after a break. Some commercials offer a complex of lakes and ponds, often with each water designed for a specific species or type of fishing. So if you are interested in Carp fishing there may be a dedicated lake. There may also be a specimen lake stocked with large fish, or a "silvers" lake stocked with species other than Carp.

Commercials often have a shop, maybe somewhere to eat, toilet facilities and parking close to the lakes. All these things can make life much easier especially when you are new to fishing.

Originally commercials were very Carp orientated with waters heavily stocked to ensure every visitor caught something. These days many commercials offer a wider range of fishing and many have reduced their stocks to improve fish health. Despite the reduction in fish numbers, many commercials report better catches than before simple because the fish are in better health.

Popular commercial fisheries can be very busy, especially in the summer. You may have to book a place in advance to fish on some lakes. If you are new to fishing then I recommend fishing a silvers lake or pleasure anglers lake until you have built up your skills. Many commercials have restrictions in place for their specimen lakes, so always check the rules first.

Generally commercials charge by the day or between set times, there may be an additional charge for night fishing as well as the number of rods you use. Some commercials will expect you to use bait bought on site, you may also have to use their nets to prevent the spread of fish disease.

Commercials offer a complete fishing package all in one convenient location, which can be good for a beginner, but I would recommend you carefully read all rules and restrictions before fishing.

Club fishing

There are fishing clubs all over the country, I have no doubt there will be one near you. They are nearly always run by volunteers on a not for profit basis. Most are members only clubs requiring an annual subscription. You may be unsure of buying a years worth of fishing in advance, but many only charge tens of pounds, go fishing more than a few times and a club can be a very economic.

Many clubs will allow you to try out their waters as a guest of someone who is already a member. Guest ticket schemes are very common among the clubs and you have the added advantage of fishing with a friend who knows the club and it's waters.

Clubs often have a good variety of lakes, ponds, rivers and streams, some man made but many will be natural. This variety can be a major advantage for you, enabling you to learn your key fishing skills much quicker.

Club waters tend to be spread out over the local area, due to waters being gained over time or when opportunities arise. They generally have no facilities of any sort so take your own bait and expect to pee in the bushes. On the up side club waters tend to have fewer restrictions on rods, bait and age of angler making club waters more accessible. You will often find you have an entire lake to yourself, club waters are much quieter than commercials, ideal if you want to learn fishing at your own pace. Club members are often quite sociable, talk to as many as possible it's a short cut to getting to know the club and it's waters.

It can be difficult to find out about a club if you don't know any members. Many clubs are decades old and fight shy of modernity, having poor websites and slow to answer email. Joining a club may require a trip to the membership secretaries house or by posting your application, few offer on-line payment methods.

Joining a club can also be a little disconcerting, you send your application in the post and a few days later your membership documents arrive. You've had no face to face contact with anyone, no one has told you where to go or what to do, you are just expected to know! Let me assure you this is quite normal, pick a water and go and have a look. You will find it all quite obvious once you get there, remember your not the first.

Free waters

These are few and far between, some local councils have free community waters and you may find one on a local common. Free water can be great, but they attract the public who like to walk their dogs and picnic which can be a distraction. The two most common things people will say to you are, "Have you caught anything yet" and "You won't catch anything here", which can get old very quickly. Still, a free water might be worth a look.

Rod licence

To fish any freshwater in the UK you must hold a valid rod licence once over twelve years of age. Find out more on the Environment Agency website or the Post Office website. Do not buy your rod licence from anywhere else.

Fishing Styles

Float fishing is a very well known method, I suspect most people imagine someone float fishing when they think of an angler. It is a very easy method to understand, a fish picks up your bait causing the float to move, you hook the fish, job done.

Ledgering is a very popular method with anglers, but not particularly well know to non-anglers. Ledgering is where your bait is held on the lake bed with a single weight, but the line is free to move (pulled by a fish) causing an indication at the rod. Special rods called quiver tips or feeder rods are used where the last foot of the rod is very flexible. When a fish picks up the bait pulling on the line, the tip of feeder rod moves indicating a fish is there.

I will tell you about both methods, but on your first trip I would recommend float fishing. It's easy to understand and is virtually guaranteed to catch fish right from the start. I will show you how to float fish with a "catch all" method, so that's any species, any size. This is ideal for a first trip, it allows you to learn basic skills and catch a few fish. A win win situation!

In recent years ledgering has become very popular with anglers who fish for Carp, ledgering is particularly suited to the way Carp feed.

Ledgering can also be a catch all method, but most anglers use it to exclude smaller fish. There is one problem with ledgering only for bigger fish, there are far fewer big fish than medium or small. If you restrict your angling to catching big Carp for example, you could spend many days fishing without catching a single fish. Big fish, being older, are much wiser than small fish making them hard to catch. Add the fact there are fewer big fish than small, you could become disillusioned or even bored of fishing before you have really begun.

For ledgering I will show you a way of fishing called the "Method feeder" which is often just called the method. The method is a way of excluding very small fish, but at the same time allow you to catch medium sized fish such as Carp.

Both float fishing and ledgering have their merits and both have their limitations, but either will catch fish on a first trip. It's entirely up to you which you try first, but to be a good all round angler you will need to master both.

Fishing Tackle

Tackle is your "tools of the trade" designed to help you catch fish. You could catch fish with just some line and a hook, free lining as it's called, but what if the fish are further out than you can throw your line. Then you need a rod to cast the hook further, casting further requires more line and something to keep it on, like a reel. How will you know when a fish is nibbling your bait, how about a float. As you can see the more you think about fishing the more equipment it appears you need. So I will go through what you need to catch fish using the two best methods to start fishing with, float fishing and ledgering.

I will start with fishing line. This may seem an odd place to start, but the tackle you use for any particular session will need to compliment and balance with the strength of the line.

Fishing line

There are dozens of different types of fishing line made from different materials all having different properties, but there are two types I would recommend, Monofilament or Copolymer. The biggest advantage to an amateur angler with both of these types of line is their knot strength. In other words the line is not dramatically weakened when tied into a knot, very important while you are still learning.

Line is described either by it's breaking strain (how much pull it takes to break) or by it's diameter. As a rule of thumb, line for use on a reel (main line) generally emphasises the breaking strain in pounds on the spool label. Whereas spools boldly marked with the lines diameter are usually for tying to the hook (hook length) which is then tied to the main line. Spools of main line tend to come in hundreds of yards and spools of hook length line come in tens of yards.

Main line is also available in different colours with white, brown, green and red being common. I have not noticed an advantage of one colour over another, but I must admit I use brown for ledgering, green or white (clear) for float fishing. Red line is claimed to be invisible in water due to the way the red part of the light spectrum penetrates water.

If you are buying line for the very first time as a newbie angler, a good starting point is 250 yards of white 4lb main line for float fishing and 250 yards of white or brown 8lb line for ledgering.

Over time your line will get damaged and degrade ultimately weakening it to a point where it can no longer be relied upon. Look to completely replace your line at least once a year and store it out of sunlight between fishing trips.

Float rod

Float fishing is generally a sensitive method of fishing using light lines and a rod to suite. Matching the rod to the line (or vice versa) is important, using a stiff rod with light line will cause problems when playing a fish. A rod and line should compliment and balance each other, as should all the tackle in the set-up.

If you took my advice you will be using 4lb main line. Float rod specifications often state the range of line strengths the rod is designed for. Look for a two or three section rod between 11 and 13 feet long with a range of line strengths that include 4lb. A rod with a 3lb to 6lb range will be ideal. Float rods can also be described as light, medium or heavy, in this case go for medium.

Carbon fibre is the most common material used to make modern rods, it's a tried and tested material, given a choice play safe and select carbon fibre. The handle should be in one piece, rods with two small handles are not float rods. The rings on the rod should stand well out from the rod keeping the light line away from the shaft.

Ledger rod

There are two types of ledger rod, one with a very flexible tip called a feeder or quiver tip and rods with standard tip called bomb rods or simply ledger rods. In this book I will only be dealing with feeder rods, they are ideal for the beginner and offer one of the best ways to catch fish.

Feeder rods are sold by how much weight they can cast, line strength is perhaps a secondary factor, but still plays a part. Buying a feeder rod is a bit of a mine field, there are hundreds of rods to choose from. A rod of ten or eleven feet long that will cast 40g to 90g with a line capacity of up to 8lb should handle everyday fishing on small lakes and ponds. May also be described as a "medium" feeder rod. Many feeder rods come with two or three different tips or top sections, stiff, medium and light are common, designed to be used in different conditions.

General purpose reel

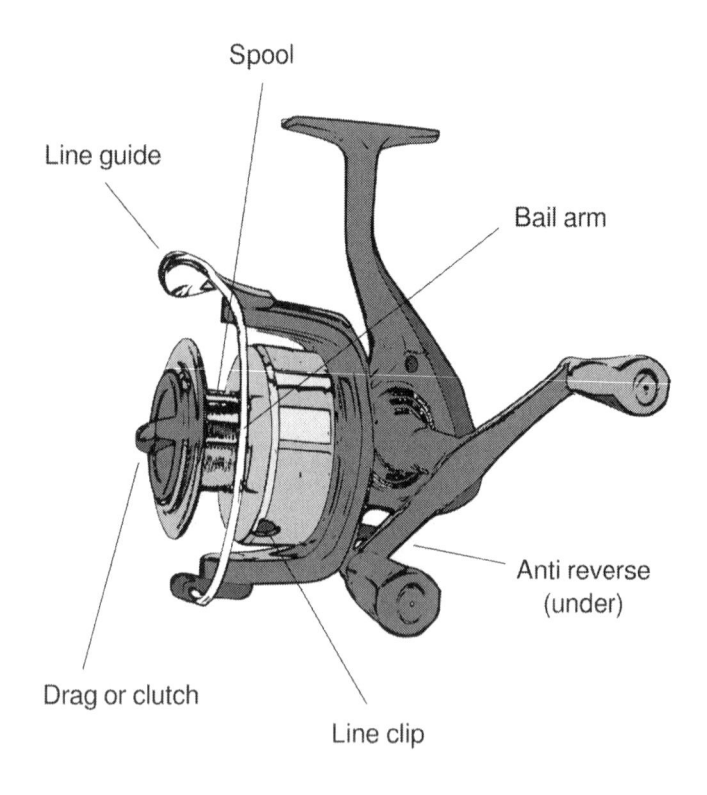

Spool
Line guide
Bail arm
Anti reverse (under)
Drag or clutch
Line clip

Fixed spool reel

I recommend a fixed spool reel, size 30 or 40 often referred to as 3000 or 4000. The number may include the letters "FD" meaning front drag or "RD" meaning rear drag. The drag on a reel is a clutch system that releases line if the fish you're playing pulls hard or runs. The rod is designed to absorb short lunges from the fish. But if you hook something big the drag is designed to smoothly let line out in a controlled way, allowing the fish to run without breaking the line. The drag resistance can be adjusted by a knob, either on the front (FD) or rear (RD) of the reel. Generally float fishing reels have front drag, rear drag reels were made to allow adjustment to the drag resistance while playing a fish. I like to use front drag reels for all my fishing, but it's a personal choice. Quite a few reels come with a spare spool, sometimes a shallow spool for light line. As a first reel I would be tempted to get one with at least one standard spool and one shallow. Finally, there's a lot of bluster about materials and the number of bearings, don't get too wrapped up in all that, any reel costing £30 plus should be fine.

How it works

No doubt there will be a leaflet with your reel explaining how it works, but I thought it might be of use to go through it in plain English.

The spool

The spool holds the main line, shallow spools are for light line and deep spools are for heavy line. Each spool should have how much line it can hold written on it, usually shallow spools are for float fishing and deep spools for ledgering.

Bail arm

The bail arm ensures the line is moved to the line guide at one end of the arm which guides the line onto the spool when you turn the handle to wind line in.

The Handle

No prizes for guessing what the handle does, but if you can, get a reel with a double handle. Modern reels are very free running, with a single handle the weight of the handle can turn the reel as the handle moves to hang down. This always happens when you're not looking and can cause the line to slacken and wrap it self round the reel body, just before you get a bite from the fish of a lifetime. If you are right handed the handle should be on the left side of the reel when on the rod, swap the handle to the right if you are left handed.

The drag or clutch

When you hook a big fish (notice I say when not if) the fish will tear off across the lake with surprising power. The drag on your reel is designed to let line out in a controlled way as the fish runs. The spool will rotate as the fish pulls letting out line, the line passes over the line guide and up through the rod rings. The rod is designed to absorb the initial lunge of the fish and the reel takes over as the fish runs further. Without a clutch the fishes power would quickly exceed the strength of line causing it to break. The fish would still have a hook in it's mouth and be tethered to a length of line, this is bad.

The reel will have a drag adjuster either on the front of the spool or on the back end of the reel body. Setting the amount of resistance offered by the drag is set by tightening or loosening the adjuster. Often the adjuster on a front drag reel also holds the spool on, requiring you to set the drag resistance every time you change the spool. Some reels have overcome this by having the drag mechanism built into the spool with a simple release button to change spools.

The drag resistance should be set lower than the line strength ensuring the clutch slips before the line breaks.

Lets imagine you have line or a hook length of 4lb, the clutch must begin to slip with a pull of less than 4lb, say 3lb. There is another factor to take into account, with the fish running the rod is pulled round into a curve with the line tight against the rod rings. This will offer an additional 1lb or more of resistance, which must be added to the overall resistance. So with 4lb line the reel clutch must be set to no more than 2lb. To be sure I would set the reels drag at 1lb 8oz, this may not sound much but rest assured when we cover playing a fish all will become clear. Use a spring balance to pull against the drag and measure when the clutch slips, if you don't have a spring balance use your judgement airing on the side of caution.

Anti reverse

When turned on, this feature only allows you to reel line in. When turned off you can turn the handle to reel line in or let line out. When playing a fish the anti reverse should be on preventing the reel spinning out of control when the fish runs. I usually switch on anti reverse as soon as I have cast my line out so I'm ready to go as soon as I get a bite.

Loading line onto your reel

The spool

The spools that came with your reel will be marked with their line capacity. Shallow spools are for fine light lines as used in float fishing and deep spools are for heavy thicker line often used for ledgering. Although a spool may be marked to take 200 yards of 8lb line, there is nothing to stop you loading the spool with 400 yards of 4lb line, but this does seem a bit wasteful.

A spool is considered loaded when the line fills the spool to just below the front lip. If your reel does not have a shallow spool for light lines, you can use a deep spool if you pack it out first. Use cheap or old line to pack the spool, once it's about half full wrap a turn or two of tape over the packing to finish.

Loading the line

To load the line you will need your reel, a rod, a bowl of water and a pot of jam. Take the butt section of your rod and attach the reel, pass the new line down through the rings of the rod towards the reel.

Arbor knot

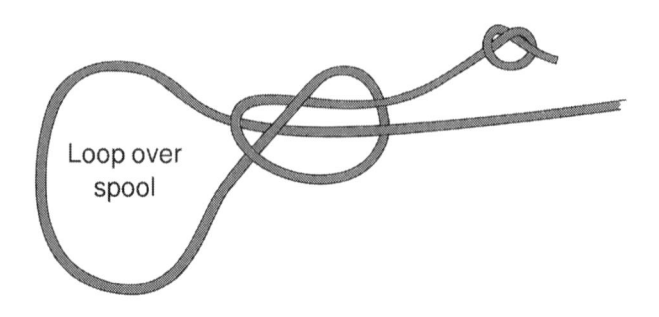

Tie a overhand knot in the end of the line. Moisten the knot before you pull it tight and cut the tail off short. Next tie a overhand knot around the main line a few inches up, then moisten and tighten. You should now have a loop of line to slip over the spool as shown above.

Open the bail arm by pulling it up over the spool, pass the loop of line over the spool and pull the line to tighten the loop down onto the spool. A little pulling back and forth might be required to close the loop down tight.

Close the bail arm and turn on the anti reverse.

Sink the new spool of line into the bowl of water with the label uppermost, place the pot of jam on top to hold the spool in place.

Hold the rod over the bowl of water with the end rod ring above the spool of new line. Hold the shaft of the rod with one hand and turn the reel handle with the other. The line must be loaded under tension, allow the line to pass under your index finger and apply tension to the line as passes. It's difficult to quantify the tension required, but enough to ensure the line lays neat and flat on the reel. In other words some tension but not too much. The new line is made wet as it's drawn from the bowl of water, this is done to reduce the possibility of getting a friction burn or cut on your index finger applying the tension.

To reduce twisting the line as it's loading, ensure the line is unwound from the new spool and onto the reel spool in the same direction. I have found having the new spool with the label facing up in the bowl of water is normally correct, but stop winding now and then and lower the rod tip down to see if the line curls up into loops. If it does, turn the new spool over in the bowl, wind on a little more line and check again. But you should find the spool in the bowl is label up most of the time.

Using the above method greatly reduces the chance of twisting the line as it's loaded onto the reel. If the line is allowed to get twisted it will cause no end of problems with tangles while fishing.

With the reel now loaded and ready to use, lets look at the rest of the tackle.

Floats shot and accessories

Waggler floats

Waggler is a general term for a float that is fixed to the line at the bottom end only. There are loaded and unloaded, a loaded waggler has some weight built in to the bottom to help set the float. An unloaded waggler is more practical than loaded, ask for an unloaded straight insert waggler float.

An unloaded straight insert waggler looks like a pencil with a slimmer inserted orange end, the float body will be made of clear plastic or painted black, either is fine. If there is a selection go for the middle sizes, 4BB (2AAA) to 8BB (4AAA) two of each. There are many types of waggler, but start with an unloaded straight insert waggler for your first days in fishing.

Shot dispenser

Shot dispensers are simply containers of non toxic weights which are used on the line to set or "cock" the float.

Hooks

I suggest you use hooks ready tied to nylon (mono) at first. A size 22 hook is very small a 10 is much bigger, essentially the larger the number the smaller the hook. For float fishing a pack of size 18 and a pack of size 16 round bend barbless spade end hooks should do to begin with. An 18 can be used with one or two maggots, and a 16 is good for slightly bigger baits like sweetcorn. Make sure the line they are tied to is 4lb or less. Hooks for ledgering will be discussed in the ledgering section.

Disgorger

A disgorger is used to unhook a fish you have caught and is a must have piece of equipment. If you ever have trouble unhooking a fish, just ask another angler for help. If possible get a standard disgorger and a Slammo disgorger.

Small artery forceps

Used to remove hooks too large for a disgorger.

Baiting needle

A special needle for attaching bait to the hook length of a ledger rig.

Loop tyer

A simple plastic device to tie small neat loops in fishing line.

Plummet

A plummet is used in conjunction with a float to find out how deep the water is. You should always know what's in front of you before you start fishing. This will be covered later.

Catapult

Simply used to fire out free offerings to the fish.

Landing net

This is the net used to scoop the fish from the water. A 20 to 24 inch round or spoon shaped net with knotless mesh will do.

Landing net handle

Landing nets and handles screw together, any landing net should fit any handle. A 2 metre long handle will be long enough to use on most lakes and ponds.

Unhooking mat

Similar to a baby changing mat, but is used to lay fish on while you remove the hook. Many clubs and commercials insist anglers have and use an unhooking mat.

Other equipment

There is no end of other equipment you can take with you, in fact some anglers use a barrow to carry all their tackle down to the water.

Here is a list of items worth considering.

Tackle box or bag

You will need something to carry all your tackle and bait. At first a bag will probably do, but if you get hooked on fishing there's a good chance you will end up with a box and several bags!

Something to sit on

You could sit on a chair, your tackle box, a seat box or the ground. Personally I like to take a chair, mine has mud feet and adjustable legs to account for uneven ground. When I first started I used a tackle box strong enough to sit on, which can be bought for tens of pounds. A seat box (as the name suggests) is designed to sit on but also has adjustable legs and compartments for all your tackle, these can cost hundreds of pounds.

Clothing

It's important to protect yourself from the elements, not just the cold but also hot summer days. In the summer cover your skin, long sleeve shirt, trousers and a hat to protect you from direct sun light. If the sun is in front of you remember the sunlight will reflect off the water, you will get a double dose, from above and in front. At the other extreme winter temperatures can quickly chill you to the bone. Wear layers in the cold, a base layer, a middle layer and a water proof, wind proof outer layer. Thermal socks, boots, hat or balaclava will help to keep you warm.

Polarised sunglasses

Reduce glare and eye strain on bright and sunny days.

Metalwork

Ledgering and some float fishing require the rod to be held steady in rod rests. One piece rod rests are available, or preferably two metal bank sticks. Bank sticks have a threaded top into which you can screw various attachments, rests, bait trays, camera adaptors and all manor of additions.

Umbrella

Ideal to keep the sun, rain or wind off. Fishing umbrellas don't have a handle, they have a spike which is pushed into the ground and a loop in the top to attach a guide line.

Luggage

Luggage has become very popular, rod bags, bait bags, bags for your nets, there seems to be a piece of luggage for everything. The only one you may need in the early days is a rod bag. Rod bags often have a place for a fishing umbrella and bank sticks.

A towel

Very handy for keeping your hands dry and to wipe off fish slime.

A bucket

Use a bucket to mix ground bait or method mix.

Bait

Hook bait and feed

It's often assumed that anglers just put bait on the hook, cast in and wait. Although this does work, you are relying on a fish to first notice your hook bait and then be hungry enough to eat it. Using this single hook bait method will catch fish, but only a few.

A more productive method is to attract a number of fish into your swim with some feed. It's like feeding birds in the garden, at first you will see one or two birds, but after a while dozens will turn up.

Feed

Generally small particles of food are used as feed, maggots, small fish pellets, seeds, grain and liquidised bread are all good examples. Bait manufacturers sell ready made bags or tins of feed which you can use straight from the packet.

Bags of fish pellets are sold by their size, 2mm or 3mm are a good size to use as feed. Seeds and grains can also be bought off the shelf, commonly referred to as particle bait. Never use dried beans or seeds from the supermarket as feed until they have been cooked or soaked.

Dried seeds slowly expand when wet, if a fish eats a handful of dried seeds they will expand inside the fishes stomach resulting in the death of the fish, this is bad. Please only use particle baits that have been properly prepared.

Maggots are a well know and popular bait, sold in pints maggots can be bought loose in tackle shops and some garden centres. Maggots can be used for both feed and on the hook, they are eaten by just about every species of fish.

Liquidised bread is just that, fresh white bread with the crusts removed and put through a liquidiser, squeezed into balls the size of a conker.

There must be hundreds of different foods that can be used as fish feed, but always remember the point is to attract lots of fish into your swim. Don't feed the fish too much because if they feed their fill they will wander off, little and often is the key with feed.

All of these loose feeds can be thrown in to the lake by hand or with a catapult. Try to hit the same spot with your feed to keep the fish together.

Ground bait

One problem with loose feed is that you can't throw it very far, either because it is quite light, or because it spreads out too much.

Originally made from bread crumb, bran, biscuit and even soil, ground bait was mixed with the loose feed and a little lake water then squeezed into balls. Balls of feed can be thrown some distance breaking up once in the water releasing the particles of feed.

The early ground baits were bland and only meant to carry loose feed. Modern ground baits are now made with flavours and colouring which also help attract the fish.

Hook bait

Once you have fish interested in your feed, offer them something tasty on the hook. Classic baits like worms, maggots and bread are much loved by fish and work all year round. Other common hook baits are sweet corn, prawns and luncheon meat cut into cubes.

Bait manufacturers offer a vast range of hook baits of every size, flavour and colour you can imagine. Coarse, Trout and Halibut pellets available in bags and pots are extremely popular and are readily eaten by fish. Ready made baits like these often come in resealable containers and will last for weeks if not months making them ideal for the amateur angler.

Mix and match

Using feed and bait that compliment each other can be very effective. Hemp and sweetcorn, maggots and worms, liquidised bread and flakes of bread are all good examples. Putting hemp and cubes of luncheon meat together also works because both are loved by fish. You can feed with more than one type of particle, hemp and pellets or hemp, pellets, barley bound together with ground bait. The possibilities are endless and it's always worth experimenting.

Casting

Casting a line is one of those skills people either do naturally or have to practice, I was in the latter group. On the up side, because it did not come naturally to me I had to work out how to cast and understand what went wrong when I'm pulling my line from the nearest tree. As it turns out it's not too difficult to cast accurately to the same spot over and over, it's more about rhythm.

Find a place you can practice, a field or quiet part of the lake. Use your float rod with 4lb line, set the rod up and squeeze three SSG shot onto the end of the line.

Lets start with how to hold a rod, the trick is to position your hand so that when you grip the rod your index finger can reach the front lip of the reel spool. I find I can reach the spool comfortably with the foot of the reel between my little finger and ring finger, I notice others can reach with the reel foot between middle and ring fingers, the important thing is to be able to reach the spool comfortably. I always use two hands to cast, being right handed I hold the rod in my right hand and hold the bottom of the handle with my left. For float fishing and ledgering a two handed cast is the usual way.

Stand or sit as you prefer, but practice casting from both positions. Hold the rod so that you can see the weight in front of you, reel in or reel out until the weight hangs at about half way between your hand and the tip of the rod. Hook the line with your index finger (rod hand) at right angles to the spool and open the bail arm with your free hand. If the weight falls to the floor adjust the way you hook the line with your finger and try again.

With the line held behind your finger and the bail arm open, move the rod round slightly to your side swinging the weight around with it and continue in one smooth movement until the rod and weight arrive behind you. Sweep the rod forwards catapulting the weight with it, it should feel as if you are throwing the weight with the hand that holds the reel and the rod butt pivots on your other hand. Just as the rod approaches vertical release the line from under your index finger and the weight should be flung out with line pulling off the spool. Watch the weight as it flies through the air and point the rod tip roughly at it as it goes. As the weight approaches the water, in the last second, lightly touch the lip of the spool with your index finger to slow the speed of line coming off the reel, don't stop the line, let it flick under your finger. This is called "feathering the line", which allows any slack line to be tightened and also causes a lighter landing of the weight on the water.

The most important and perhaps the most difficult part of casting is to perform the casting action all in one smooth movement with no stops or jerks. On this your very first cast, when you sweep the rod forwards, do so with a positive action but not so that the rod makes a loud swish. If the casting weight is within the capacity of the rod, swishing will not be necessary.

I like to think your first cast sent the weight twenty yards, but what if it did not cast as expected, here are some common faults.

The weight hit the water just in front

If the weight shot straight down like an arrow and splashed into the water, you released the line too late. If the weight went way up into the air and came down with a plop, then you released the line too early. Try again ensuring the weight is half way between the rod tip and your hand when you start, it's very important at this stage that the weight is always within a couple of inches of half way. Roughly line the weight up against a rod ring or the joint of the rod if it helps, but always start with the same amount of "drop".

Hook the line with your finger, open the bail arm and smoothly cast again. Release the line at a slightly different time to correct the cast. Keep adjusting your technique until the weight follows a nice arc (trajectory) in the air and lands twenty yards away.

Correct your aim

Choose a target on the far bank to aim at, a tree or something on the opposite bank. Imagine a line between you and the target, practise casting and try to land the weight on the line. Don't worry about distance, just try to aim straight.

If you find your weight constantly lands to the left of your line, it means you are sweeping the rod forward too soon. Bring the rod further behind you on the back swing before sweeping the rod forwards.

If you find your weight constantly lands to the right of your line (a common problem), there are two possible faults. Either you are sweeping the rod forward too late, or you are pausing for a split second before you sweep forwards. Pausing the rod behind you doesn't stop the weight continuing to swing. In the split second you pause, the weight will swing round too far, sweeping forwards at that point will always cause the weight to land to the right of your line even if the rod is on the correct path.

To correct aim, the back swing and sweep forwards must be one smooth action, the timing of the sweep forwards can then be adjusted earlier or later to fine tune your aim.

Distance

Casting the same distance every time simply requires practice, there are no short cuts or adjustments to cast technique that will guarantee distance. Some reels do have a line clip designed to stop the weight at the same distance on every cast, but I would recommend learning correct technique before using the line clip.

Your first fishing trip

Where on the lake to fish

Most lakes have clearly defined areas of bank from which to fish called a swim, marked with a numbered stake hammered into the ground called a peg. Each swim will include all the water in front extending half way across and halfway to the swims either side. You can fish further out than half way if the swim opposite is empty. Fishing into another angers swim is bad etiquette and will cause friction, so please don't.

Deciding where on a lake to fish when it's your first attempt can be difficult. True you could just pick any swim and hope for the best, but there are a few clues you can use.

Before you leave

Have a look at their website, there may be a gallery of catch photos that indicate where fish were caught and perhaps which baits was used. If it's a club website, the club will often put their best waters at the top of their waters list, so look at these first. Match fishing results can also indicate the better pegs and waters. If there is a members forum this too can yield valuable Information.

At the lake

Some pegs at the lake will be worn down to the bare earth with no weeds or grass, even if the swim is fished from a platform the path leading to it may be well trodden. This wear and tear indicates the swim is very popular with anglers. There are two main reasons for this, either this genuinely is a good place to fish, or it's easy to get to, near the car park for example. Either way a popular swim will have more bait thrown into it than a less popular one. The fish know they can always rely on food in these areas, but they also know that they may get caught so will be more cautious. A worn swim is a good place to spend your first fishing session.

Features

Overhanging trees, reeds, lilies and islands are all easy to see fish holding areas. Fishing next to or against these features is often a good place to start. Underwater features can also hold fish, deep areas, shallow areas, changes in depth and different types of lake bed. On your first session though, go with the obvious features you can see, better to catch a few fish than blank.

Put it all together

In most areas you will have the choice of commercial or club fisheries, there is nothing to stop you trying several commercials or belong to more than one club.

Decide on a water, check out the website and visit the particular lake. Look for worn swims with features and talk to anyone there, you should soon get a feel for the place and the people who fish there.

On your first trip don't be too ambitious, just catch a few fish and enjoy the day. Many anglers pleasure fish like this all the time and use fishing to relax and get out into the country now and then. If you get "hooked" then there is a world of detail and complexity that will keep you occupied for a life time, you will never know it all.

Basic float rigs

The purpose of a float rig is not just to indicate a bite, but also to ensure the bait is presented to the fish in a way that looks natural. Casting out without the line getting tangled is also controlled by the rig.

There are two basic still water float rigs, the first allows the bait to sink slowly in the hope a fish will intercept the bait on it's way down. The second rig sends the bait quickly straight down to the bottom. The difference between these two rigs depends on spacing and position of the weights used to cock the float. Years ago these weights were made of lead shot as used in a shot gun, but due to the toxicity of lead it is no longer used in fishing except for the very smallest shot.

Most seven division shot dispensers contain, SSG, AAA, BB, 1, 4, 6 (non-toxic) and No.8 (lead) shot, which will be enough for either rig.

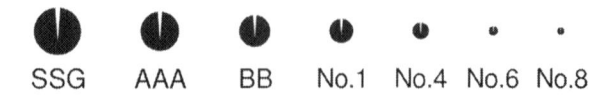

SSG   AAA   BB   No.1   No.4   No.6   No.8

To fix to your line a slot is cut into every shot, place your line in the slot and squeeze the shot to close the slot around the line.

Never use your teeth or pliers to close the shot, only ever use your fingers to avoid damaging the line and weakening it.

Slow sinking rig

First thread the float onto your main line through the loop in the base of the float, you may find the loop blocked with paint if the float is new, clear with a pin.

All floats are marked with how much weight it takes to cock them correctly, this shot capacity is described in a quantity of one size of shot, 4BB or 3AAA for example. Although shot capacity is described in this way, it's normal to use a mixture of split shot that total the floats capacity.

Lets use a 4BB float in this basic example of a slow sinking rig.

Most of the floats capacity is clustered around the base of the float, in this case three of the four BB's. This is done to ensure the base of the float is always heavier than the rest of the rig causing it to precede the rest of the rig when cast reducing the risk of a tangle. The forth BB is made up of four No 6 shot equally spaced between the float and hook. When this rig lands in the water the shot clustered around the base of the float will cause it to almost fully cock.

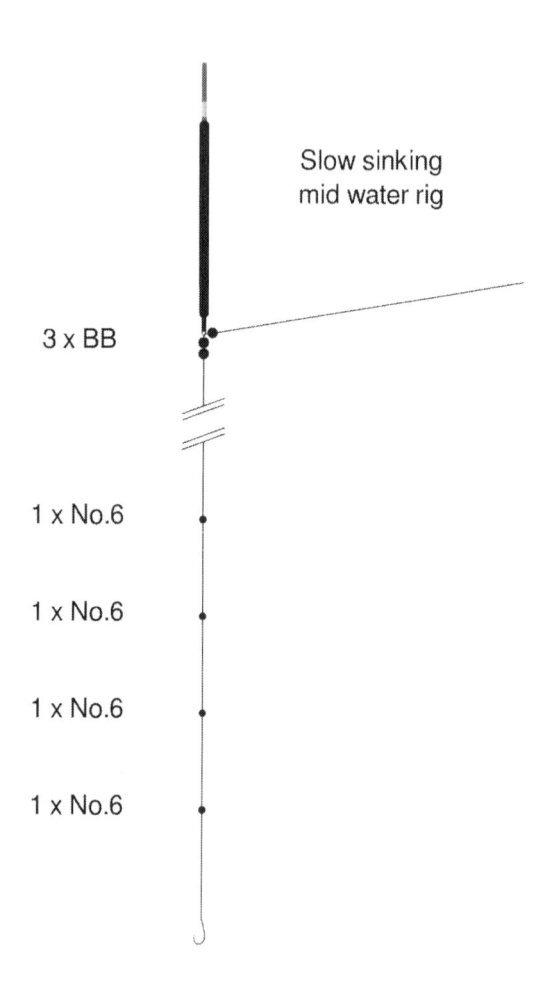

Slow sinking
mid water rig

3 x BB

1 x No.6

1 x No.6

1 x No.6

1 x No.6

The small shot below will fall slowly down through the water bringing the bait with them. As each of the small shot settle they will pull the float down a little more until only the orange tip shows above the water.

A fish could intercept the bait at any time causing one of two things to happen. Either the float will not finish cocking or the float will suddenly be pulled under as the fish swims away with the bait.

Fast sinking rig

Using the same 4BB float, we can change the position of the shot to cause the bait to fall quickly through the water straight to the bottom. Move the top two No 6's down to the second grouping them together, their combined weight will pull the bait down very quickly compared to the slow rig. But what is the point of having rigs that can sink at different speeds?

Some fish spend most of their time swimming around in the middle layers of a lake, whereas other species prefer to grub around on the bottom. The first rig is designed to catch fish from mid water and the second is designed to bypass the mid water fish in favour of the bottom dwellers.

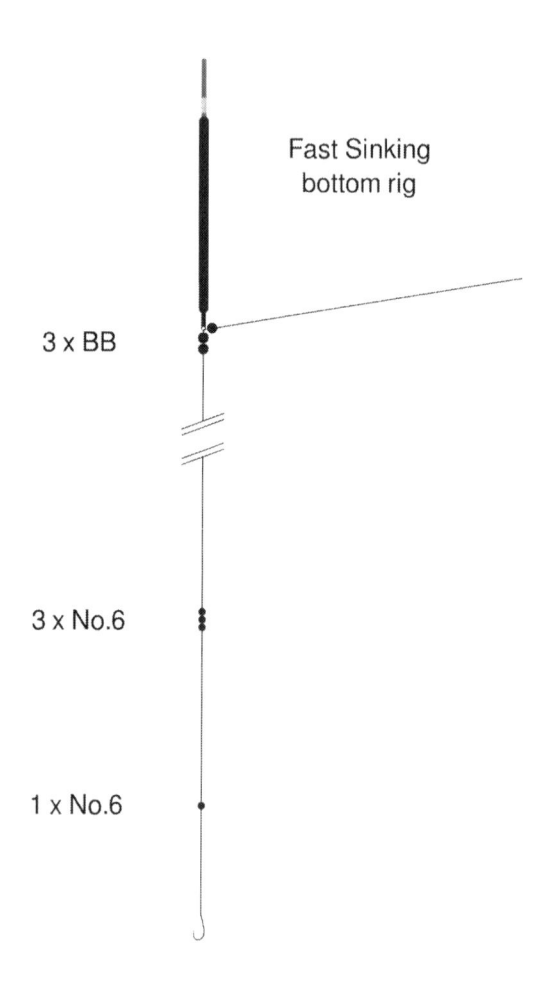

Fast Sinking bottom rig

3 x BB

3 x No.6

1 x No.6

The fast sinking rig is by far the most popular and has the advantage of targeting more species. I recommend this rig for your first float fishing trip.

So why have I bothered to show you the slow sinking rig, when the fast sinking rig is the one I recommend?

With float fishing it's all about "presentation", offering your bait in a natural way. By moving just two shots this rig behaves and presents the bait in a very different way, understanding the flexibility of float rigs is an important step in catching more fish. Deciding which to use and when is a little more complicated!

These examples both use a 4BB float which is fine for fishing in good weather at a couple of rod lengths out. Fishing further out or in windy conditions will require a heavier float both for casting and for resisting water drift caused by the wind. Please don't struggle with a very light float when a heavier one will do the job better. Heavier floats should still be set up as I have described with two thirds to three quarters of the floats capacity around the base of the float. You will have to use different split shot than above down the line, but always use a No 6 as the weight nearest the hook. This is call the "Tell tale shot" or the "Working Shot", it's this last shot that is disturbed when a fish picks up your bait.

A No 6 is light enough not to cause suspicion by the fish, but heavy enough to cause the float to move which is just what we want.

Anglers have written entire books on float fishing and like many topics in angling it can get very complicated to a point that is no longer helpful. As a beginner I would say to you, learn the key skills first, master these rig because they will catch most of your fish.

Setting up your tackle

Once you have found a peg to fish, the next task is to get all your tackle ready. Ensure your seat is level and comfortable and there is room around you to layout your equipment. Look around you to see if there are any obstacles that will get in the way of casting or playing a fish. If you can, remove any twigs or debris in the water in front of you, it's easy for your landing net to get caught up while you are trying to land a fish.

Before you do anything else, screw your landing net into the handle and lay it down on the bank with the end of the handle in reach from your seat. I always do this first, it's easy to forget when you are eager to start fishing, I have done it myself discovering my blunder as I try to land the first fish.

Push one bank stick into the bank at the edge of the water, push the second to your right (if you are right handed) and a little behind your seat, screw in the front and rear rod rests.

Assemble the rod ensuring all the rings are in line. Attach the reel with the spool of 4lb line and open the bail arm, thread the line through the centre of every ring and pull through some slack. Close the bail arm, switch on the anti reverse and place the rod in it's rests.

At this point you need to choose which float to use, as you learn more about fishing you will be able to make an informed decision based mainly on weather conditions. As this is your first trip I will suggest you use a 3AAA straight inset waggler, this is a versatile float which will work in all but the roughest of conditions.

Thread the float up the line three of four feet and squeeze just one AAA split shot either side of the float. Don't add the rest of the weights just yet, tie a loop knot in the end of the main line for attaching the hook length.

My favourite loop knot is the figure of eight loop knot, I have always found this to be an excellent knot that won't slip or weaken the line too much. Please don't be tempted to use an overhand loop knot as it does weaken Monofilament quite considerably.

Figure of eight loop knot

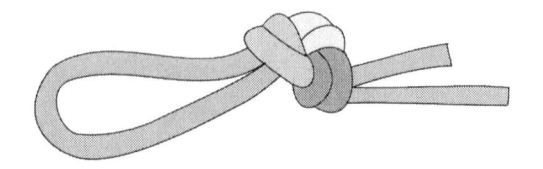

Alternatively use a loop tyer to create the loop.

I will assume you have some ready made hook lengths. Select a size 16 hook tied to weaker breaking strain line than the 4lb main line. The hook length should always be weaker than the main line, so that if a fish pulls very hard and breaks the line, it will only break the weaker hook length. That way you don't loose your float and weights and the fish won't be towing your tackle around the lake, which would be bad.

To attach the hook length, pass the main line loop through the loop on the hook length and then pass the hook through the main line loop. This is the best and strongest method to attach the hook length, I call it the through and through method.

Loop to loop

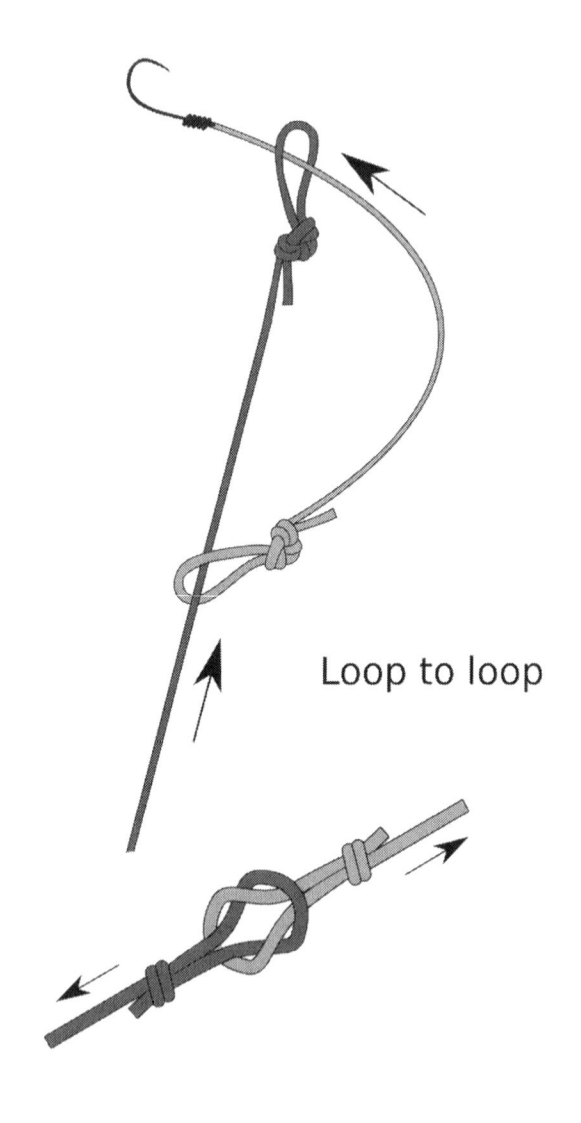

Plumbing the depth

Deciding exactly where in front of you to fish can be difficult, especially if you are looking at a featureless sheet of water. If there is a reed bed or lilies then these are good fish holding areas, but casting to an island can be difficult and I would avoid that this time. Look for a spot you can cast beyond and then reel the float back to that same spot each time. Feeding and fishing in the same place will increase your chances of catching. Please don't be too ambitious with distance, fish will visit all parts of a lake, there is no need to cast miles, two or three rod lengths out will be enough.

Knowing the depth of the water in front of you is very important when float fishing and very useful with other methods. To start, drop your line in as it is, because we have not put enough weight under the float yet it should be poking right out of the water or even laying flat. Bring the line back in to attach the plummet.

With a standard cone shaped plummet, pass the hook through the loop in the top and press the hook point into the cork base. The plummet is much heavier than the floats capacity, so in the water the float will either be sunk by the plummet if the water is deep, or the float will bob up as you saw a moment ago if the water is shallow.

Cast the plummet out just beyond your chosen spot. If the float disappears under the water, the amount of line between the plummet and the float is too little, in other words the water is deeper. The float needs to be moved further away from the plummet. If the float bobs up or lays flat on the surface, the distance between plummet and float is too great, the water is shallow, move the float closer to the plummet. Don't reel in straight away though, reel in a few feet and let the float settle again. If you could not see the float before and now you can, the water is shallower in this new spot, there has been a change in depth over just a few feet. Unsurprisingly most lakes and ponds get shallower closer to the bank, but some have a sudden step up whereas other have a gradual incline. Finding a step in the lake bed is a good thing, natural food will collect at the bottom of any step and so will the fish. So even if you have a featureless sheet of water in front, finding a step in the lake bed is a feature you can fish against. Cast out and draw back a few feet at a time all over the water in front to about three rod lengths out, try to get a mental picture of the contours in the lake bed.

The point of all this is to work out the depth of water in a spot that has a feature the fish are naturally attracted to. I know this all seems a bit of a faff when all you want to do is get fishing, but I assure you fishing in the right place will catch you more fish more often than a guess.

What if there are no viable features and the lake bed simply deepens slowly away into infinity? This is rare, most places have some feature or other, but if your swim doesn't you have two choices. With your rod set up for testing the depth, have a look at other available swims to find one that does have features such as changes in depth. Or you can make your own feature by putting in several balls of ground bait laced with feed which the fish can home in on.

Once you have chosen the exact spot you want to fish, the next task is to set the float at exactly the right depth. The aim is for the hook with it's bait to just touch bottom once the float has settled. Cast to your chosen spot and see how the float sits, reel in and adjust the float up and down the line until the plummet pulls the float down to show half an inch of the top. When shot was made of lead anglers could slide the shot up and down the line to adjust the position of the float. Modern shot is harder and may damage the line so I always remove the shot and squeeze it back on in a new place.

Once you have the float in just the right place, remove the plummet and place the hook in a hook hold on or near the handle of the rod. Some rods have a metal loop for the hook just above the handle, otherwise hook onto the first ring.

Engage the reels anti reverse and wind in until the line goes tight, now make one last adjustment to the floats position on the line. Move the float one inch closer to the hook. This is done because cone shaped plummets always land on the lake bed on their side and the lake bed will have a layer of soft mud or silt that the plummet will sink into. Moving the float a little will take account of these.

Finally hold the float pointing up the rod and mark where the top of the float comes against the rod shaft. I like to use a chinagraph pencil for this, if needed, this mark is used to reset the floats depth without the trouble of having to re-plumb.

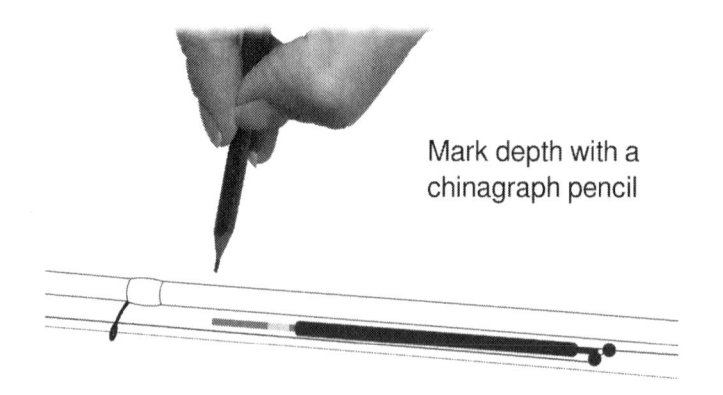

Mark depth with a chinagraph pencil

Finish shotting the float

At the moment we only have a AAA either side of the float, to cock the float correctly the rest of the shot must be added, but which shotting pattern to use, slow or fast sinking?

There are two main factors to consider, species of fish you want to catch and time of year. Some fish are designed to feed on the bottom, Tench and Bream for example. Whereas Rudd feed in the upper layers and off the surface, they have an upturned mouth designed for the job. Yet other species are opportunists and will eat off the top, on the bottom and at any layer, Carp are a good example.

All still water fish feed in the summer, but in the depths of winter the species that prefer grubbing around on the bottom tend not to feed. Tench in particular seem to just vanish from the lake until the spring. Roach on the other hand will feed all year round, making them a good target in the winter. A slow sinking rig with a small hook and a single maggot or small pinch of bread is ideal for catching Roach in the cold. In the summer I might use a slow sinking rig to catch only Roach and Rudd in the upper layers. Use the slow rig primarily to catch fish that spend most of their time in the mid to upper layers of the water, or when other species are put off by the cold. I suspect the fast rig will be of more interest to you, so lets start with that.

Fast sinking, bottom rig

Earlier we set up a 3AAA float with just one AAA either side on 4lb main line with a size 16 hook. To complete this as a bottom rig, start by squeezing one No.6 shot on to the line six inches from the hook. Don't worry if the shot is on the weaker hook length, so long as you only use your fingers to squeeze the shot on it will be fine. Next add a bulk of three No.4 shot ten inches above the tell tale No.6. The second weight up the line must always be further from the tell tale than the tell tale is from the hook, this helps prevent tangles on the cast.

Cast your rig out to water that is as deep or deeper than the spot you set the rig up for earlier. Often the float capacity written on the float is only a guide, you may find the float has an inch or more of tip showing or it has sunk out of site. Add or remove shot to the bulk until the float cocks with half an inch showing above the water.

Fishing on the bottom

With all your tackle laid out, the drag on the reel set and your fast sinking bottom rig set up, it's time to try and catch some fish.

The first job is to attract some fish to the spot you've chosen, start by throwing or catapulting some loose feed to that spot. Look to keep the feed within an area the size of an average dinner table. Start with a small handful or half a catapult pouch of whatever loose feed you have chosen.

When baiting the hook, as a rule of thumb, the size of the hook should compliment the size of the bait. The size 16 on our rig is ideal for a single grain of sweet corn, but you could use a cube of Luncheon meat or a segment of Prawn of similar size. Very soft baits like bread or soft hook pellets can be bigger, but not excessive.

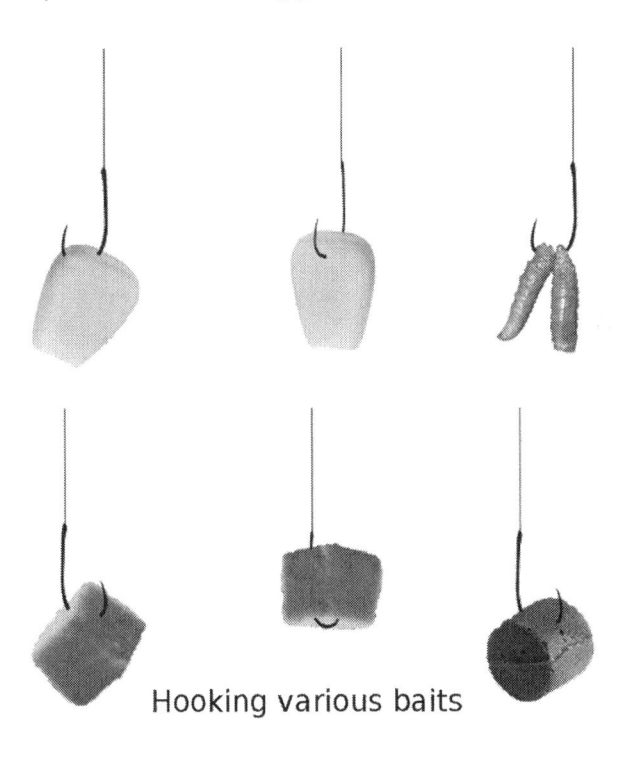

Hooking various baits

Two things should be considered when hooking the bait. Ensure the hook point is exposed unless the bait is very soft, secondly hook it in a way the bait will stay on the hook during the cast. Baits with a skin like sweetcorn and prawns will not be a problem. Semi-soft baits like Luncheon meat can fly off on the cast, to prevent this pass a baiting needle through the meat and pull the hook back through the bait. Then rotate the hook a little and pull the point of the hook into the underside of the bait. Unless the piece of meat is very soft or too big for the hook, it should stay on.

Cast out beyond your feed area, feather the line to remove any slack and cause the rig to land stretched out in a straight line away from you. Sink the rod tip below the water and reel in the float until it reaches the fed spot. The main point of sinking the rod tip is to cause the line to be pulled under the surface as you reel the float back. If the line is left on the surface, any wind or drift will cause the float to be pulled out of position, sinking the line helps prevent this. But sinking the line is not just to stop the float drifting, it also stops the bait moving along with the float. To the fish this will be the only piece of food on the move, they will be suspicious and probably won't touch it.

While you are waiting for a bite, it's important to keep feeding the fish. Put feed in at regular intervals, small handfuls of Hemp seed, micro pellets or whatever loose feed you are using should be fed every five minutes. Whether you start to catch fish or not, keep adding small amounts of feed.

The float keeps drifting

Sometimes even with the line sunk the float will still drift taking the bait with it, when fishing on the bottom a static bait is usually more productive, so we need to fix this. The easiest way is to lay the bait on the bottom in the hope this will anchor it in place. Move the float and all the split shot three inches up the line. This will mean you are fishing three inches over depth, the bait and the first three inches of line will be laying on the bottom acting as an anchor.

Still drifting ?

Move the float and shot another four inches up the line, seven inches altogether. Add a No.8 shot five inches from the hook. So now you have a No.8 at five inches, a No.6 at thirteen inches and the bulk at twenty three inches with seven inches of line and a No.8 shot on the bottom as an anchor.

It can't still be drifting !

If it is, change the No.8 for a No.6, if the rig is still moving you might want to ledger !

How do you know when a fish bites

The most obvious bite is when a fish picks up your bait and swims away with it, the float will disappear below the surface. There are other types of bite, a lift bite for example. A lift bite is when the float rises up, this happens when a fish picks up the bait and moves up in the water rather than swimming away. As the fish comes up it will lift the shot nearest the hook, the tell tale shot. Because the fish is now taking the weight of the tell tale, the float isn't, causing the float to rise. The float won't rise dramatically, it may only rise half an inch, but you can be sure it's a fish.

At times you may see the float bobbing up and down and jigging about with no clear indication, this is often tiddlers attacking the shot on the line. Or it may be small fish attacking the bait which is too big for them.

There is also a line bite which is a fish swimming into the line between the hook and float, line bites tend to cause the float to suddenly dip and then come back up to settle once more.

Generally quick sharp movements of the float are not proper bites, but do indicate the presence of fish. Slower positive movements are nearly always proper bites.

You've got a bite, now what ?

While the float is up or under the fish has the bait in it's mouth, this is the time to strike or hook the fish. To strike you need to lift the rod picking up all the line between you and the rig to cause the hook to prick the fish. Although the term "strike" implies some violence, this is not the case. Striking is a quick movement but not too hard, modern hooks are very sharp and don't need much of a pull to cause them to prick the fish, you will know immediately if you have hooked the fish.

Once hooked the object is to "play" the fish to the landing net, because playing a fish is common to all forms of fishing I will cover it as a subject on it's own later.

What to do if you don't get any bites

Lets imagine after an hour you have not caught any fish. Think about what has happened over that hour, has the float moved at all? If the float has been bobbing about but when you strike there's nothing there, that's probably small fish pecking at the shot or pecking at the bait. Keep feeding the swim, either the tiddlers will go once full of feed, or their activity will attract bigger fish into the swim.

Was the float sunk a couple of times, but once again nothing there. Almost certainly line bites, fish brushing up against the line. You have fish in the area, they are eating your feed but not the hook bait. One of several things could be wrong, the fish are suspicious of you bait, the fish don't see your bait, or they prefer to just eat the feed. The first thing to do is alter the presentation, you should have started with the bait just touching the bottom, but this may not be what the fish want. Try moving the float (just the float) three inches down the line towards the hook, this will suspend the bait three inches above the lake bed. If that doesn't work try shortening the rig another three inches, causing the bait to stop six inches above the bottom. Or how about laying the line on the bottom as you might when the float drifts as mentioned earlier.

When changing to fish shallower just move the float, when laying on the bottom move the float and shot to maintain their relationship to the bottom.

If you forget where the float was before you started moving it around, simply reset the float by offering it against the mark you made on the rod during plumbing.

Ever owned a cat? You can feed a cat the same food for a week and it will eat it every day. Then for no reason whatsoever the cat won't eat that brand of food.

It doesn't matter how long you leave it in the bowl they won't touch it, they would rather go next door and eat their cat's food.

Fish can go through cycles like this too, not only can they go off a particular food, but they can also learn a particular food comes with a cost, the cost of being caught. If possible take more than one hook bait with you, so if the fish don't fancy one, they may take another.

What if your float has not moved one bit for the hour, now you have a problem. When there are no indications at all from the float, you have no clues as to what's going on, but chances are there are no fish in the swim.

Daft as it sounds, fishing a new patch of water a few feet away can sometime make all the difference, especially in the winter when fish shoal up. So if you have been fishing to the left at a ten o'clock position, try fishing to the right at a 2 o'clock position.

If you really can't find any fish in your swim the only alternative is to move swims altogether. There could be something wrong with your first swim, perhaps it's in the sun, then try a shady swim. Perhaps you have the wind on your back, move to a swim with the wind in your face. If you have to move then move to somewhere different, there is little point moving to a swim that is much the same as the first.

On occasions no matter what you do the fish won't bite. I have been fishing on and off for forty years and even now I will get blank days. There is no shame in "having a blank", try to learn from it and put it down to experience.

Slow sinking, on the drop rig

Using the same 3AAA float as above, plumb the depths in your swim. Cluster two AAA and a BB around the float with the BB on the hook side. Add one No.8 as the tell tale shot six inches from the hook, then four No.6's equally spaced between the tell tale and the float. A No.8 is used as the tell tale to ensure the last foot or so sinks the slowest.

Look for changes in depth, even though you are fishing mid water on the drop, Roach especially like to swim above changes in depth. Use the size 18 hook with a small bait like a single maggot or a punch of bread. Large baits and large hooks tend to sink too quickly and are better suited to fishing on the bottom. A slow sinking rig is particularly effective in deeper water, six feet or more. Not only does it take the bait longer to sink, but the fish have more layers to swim in.

Slow sinking baits

Maggots work well with the slow sinking rig, loose feed half a dozen every minute or two to attract the fish. Keep feed falling through the water for the whole session and fish over the fed area. Use a single maggot as bait, hook the maggot through the fluffy looking part at the blunt end, try not to pop it!

Bread punch with liquidised white bread feed can be extremely effective. Squeeze the liquidised bread into a ball the size of a Conker to use a feed. Once in the water the ball will quickly breakup creating a cloud of bread particles fish like Roach love. To make the bread punch hook bait, cut the crusts of of several slices of fresh white bread and flatten with a rolling pin. At the water pull off small pieces of the bread to hook or use a bread punch tool. A bread punch tool is simply a hollow punch available in various diameters to cut out neat discs of bread from the flattened slice. Hook the bread through the middle and cast out, once in the water the bread will sink very slowly expanding as it goes.

How deep to fish

Mid water fish will often spend their time at a particular depth where they feel comfortable and safe. They can change depth during a day, if the sun comes out and warms the water they may come up in the water. If the weather is very cold the fish will seek out the warmest layer to swim in.

No matter what time of year or weather conditions, finding the layer they are in will improve your catch.

Start with the rig set to half the total depth of the water in front. So in six feet of water, start with the float three feet from the hook. Cast out and sink the line as described earlier, stop the float on the far side of the feed area. At a depth of three feet, It will take about twenty seconds for your rig to sink and the float to settle. Leave the float for a couple of minutes then sink your rod tip and reel the float in three or four feet. This will cause the rig to rise up in the water to sink once more giving you a second chance of catching without a recast. Repeat this process after each cast.

If the water in front is shallow (three feet or less) set the rig to finish six inches above the bottom. In such shallow water the fish have little choice of depth so should find your bait easily.

On the drop bites

Mid water fish often charge around trying to catch the feed as it falls through the water. When they take your bait the float will just get pulled under, a clear indication. Larger mid water fish don't always do this, they are in less of a hurry causing a slow positive indication at the float.

Another indication is the float doesn't fully cock, the bait has been intercepted before all the shot have come into play.

If the bait keeps getting intercepted it suggests the fish are shallower than your rig is set, shorten the distance between float and hook to place the bait amongst the fish.

If you are seeing little or no indications on the float, the fish could be deeper than your rig is fishing. Lengthen the distance between float and hook and try again.

Fish will change depth during the day with the changing conditions, but how much you feed can also cause them to change position. If the fish get very competitive for your feed, they will come up in the water to intercept the feed earlier. Increasing the frequency or amount of feed can push them back down again.

Ledgering

Simple method feeder rig

The method feeder is a wonderfully simple way of ledgering and is very popular with beginners and experienced anglers. It has the advantage of fishing itself, very little effort is required by the angler. Method feeders hold the feed, bait, hook and weight all in one neat package with no chance of getting tangles on the cast.

I find I use a 24 gram feeder the most, so get a couple of these to start with.

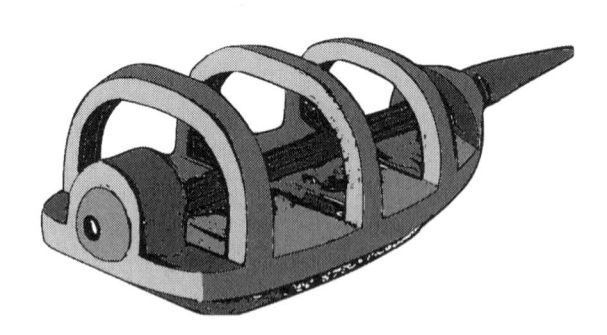

24g Method feeder

So how does the method work

A method feeder is a flat weight with a semi circular frame on top, the frame is there to hold the feed, often called method mix. The main line and a short hook length are attached to the feeder. The hook and bait are hidden inside the feed which is moulded around the feeders frame. Here's the clever bit, when cast out the feeder will always land weight down with the frame and feed uppermost. A fish when finding the feed will drop down head first to get to the food, at some point the fish will lift it's head with the hook bait and some feed in it's mouth to eat the food. As the fish lifts it's head the feeder is lifted off the lake bed, the weight of the feeder pulling on the hook length will cause the hook to prick the inside of the fishes mouth. As soon as the fish feels this hook prick it will know it's a trap and bolt, but it's too late the hook has a hold and all you need do is to reel the fish in.

Because of the way they feed, Carp are usually the target fish with the method. Other fish may be caught but Carp will fall to this trap over and over, it is a good way to catch a number of Carp in one session.

The safe method

As with any form of ledgering there is a risk that if your main line was to break while playing a fish, the fish would still have the hook in it's mouth with the feeder and main line up to the break trailing behind it. It would be very easy for the trailing line or feeder to get caught up on submerged roots, branches or reeds preventing the fish from swimming and feeding. This would mean the death of the fish. Steps must be taken to ensure this cannot happen by using the correct design of feeder and strength of line.

You must use a method feeder that can slip off the line in the event of a break. An inline method feeder has this ability because it is not fixed by a knot or any permanent method to the main line.

The main line runs through the middle of the feeder and is tied to a swivel on the far side, the line is then drawn back through the feeder until the ring of the swivel is squeezed into a rubber bush in the front of the feeder. The hook length is then attached to the other end of the swivel, this hook length must be made of line weaker than the main line.

First steps in fishing

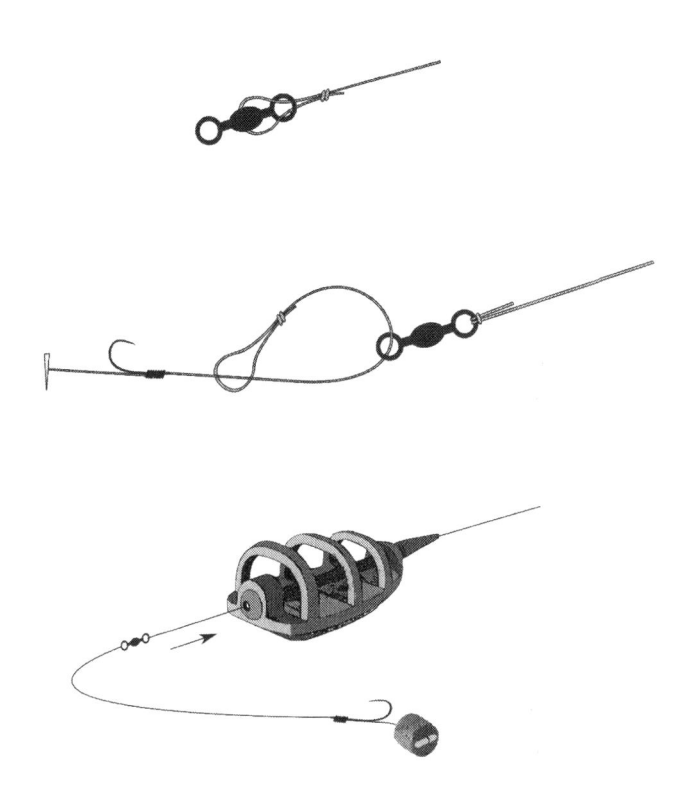

Method feeder rig

Lets imagine you hook a big fish that charges off across the lake towards a reed bed. If you try hard to stop the fish running the line will break, but with your rig tied correctly, the weaker hook length will break first.

The fish will only have a hook and a few inches on line in its mouth which will not prevent it swimming or feeding. As for the hook, it will eventually fall out so long as it's a barbless hook. The main line should not break being stronger than the hook length, but assuming the worst and the main line does break, the fish will be tethered to a heavy method feeder, but not for long. Very quickly the feeder will be knocked off the tight fitting swivel in the front and the broken main line will pull free leaving the feeder on the lake bed. Even if the fish makes it to the reeds, the feeder will get pulled off by the reed stems as the fish crashes through them.

The Hook length

For the method feeder to work effectively, the hook must prick the fishes mouth. Unlike float fishing the bait cannot be mounted on the hook, nothing should get in the way of the hook point. Instead the bait is attached below the hook on a short piece of line called a hair.

When the line is tied to the hook the loose end is not cut short, instead it is used as a way of attaching the bait leaving the hook exposed. When the fish picks up the bait the hook comes with it, it's then just a matter of the bare

Hair rig

hook pricking the fishes mouth causing the fish to bolt.

Hook lengths are available ready made, go for hook sizes of 12 and 14, four inches long and with a hair. Attaching the bait to the hair can be achieved in a number of ways depending on the bait used. A soft bait like Luncheon meat or sweet corn can be attached by passing the hair through the bait, but hard baits like pellets are best attached by an small elastic band.

Method feeder baits

There is a school of thought that says the hook bait is of little importance when fishing the method, simple because the fish sucks in everything on the feeder including the bait. Personally I feel it can't hurt to have a bait that compliments the feed, or a bait you know the fish will eat.

As it is the feed that initially attracts the fish, care must be taken in selecting and preparing the feed. There are three main types of feed used, method mix which is a powder, often quite course, which is dampened to allow it to be formed around the feeder. The second is micro pellets which when damp stick together and can be moulded on to the feeder. The third is just mixing the first two, method mix and pellets.

There is a vast range of ready made micro pellets and method mix, all are quite easy to use with instructions on the packet. To start with use a standard method mix of whatever flavour you fancy, if in doubt look for an "original flavour" mix, you can be sure an original mix has been well and truly tested and works. Once you are happy with mixing and using method mix, move on to micro pellets for a few sessions.

Popular feeder hook baits are Luncheon meat, sweetcorn, pellets, boilies or an imitation bait made of rubber. The one thing they all have in common is that they are all roundish or squarish and between 8mm and 10mm in size. I suspect the most popular bait is the boilie, but what is a boilie?

Boilies

A boilie is a paste bait formed into balls then boiled in water for a few seconds, this has the effect of cooking the paste making it stiffer and with a harder shell. Boilies last for hours underwater and cannot easily be pecked apart by small fish. Boilies are available in hundreds of colours and flavours in sizes from 10mm to 22mm, but for the feeder I like to use 10mm boilies.

Attaching the hook bait

As mentioned above, the hook bait is not on the hook but hangs below the hook on a hair, there are several ways to attach the bait to the hair, we will look at the two easiest.

Quickstop

This is a very simple device tied to the end of the hair which will work with any soft bait. The Quickstop is pushed through the bait with a Quickstop needle which fits into one end. Once through the Quickstop is turned at right angles to the hair, the bait is then pushed down tight against the stop.

Pellet band

The pellet band is a small latex ring tied to the hair which is stretched around a hard bait like an 8mm pellet. It's not difficult to stretch the band around a pellet with your finger, or you can use a pellet band tool.

Set up for feeder fishing

As with float fishing, layout your equipment within easy reach and attach the landing net to it's handle. Push one bank stick in at the waters edge to one side of your position and the second just in front of your chair on the opposite side. Arrange the bank sticks so that the rod is roughly parallel to the bank in front of you, but easily in reach. If the fish are hungry with bites coming quickly, it is easier to place the rod in the front rest and hold the butt in your lap.

Preparing the feed

Although there will be instructions on the packet, I will quickly run through preparing the feed.

Method mix

Pour the dry method mix into a bucket, add small amounts of lake water and mix thoroughly. Keep adding water a little at a time until the mix can be squeezed into balls, leave the mix to soak for 15 minutes. It's a good idea to mix the feed first and set-up your tackle while it's soaking. Add a little more water if required before you start fishing.

Micro pellets

The light coloured 2mm Coarse pellets are a good choice and seem to work all year round, they are rock hard straight from the bag and will need twenty minutes to prepare. Two thirds fill a maggot bait box with pellets and cover with lake water, ensure all the pellets get wet. Then immediately put the lid on the bait box and turn the box over to drain the excess water through the hole in the lid, leave for ten minutes upside down draining. After ten minutes, turn the box the right way up and allow the pellets to stand for a further ten minutes. The pellets should now be soft enough to stick together when squeezed.

Loading the feeder

You can just mould the feed around the feeder with your hands, but all the manufacturers have ready made moulds for their feeders.

Lay the hook and bait in the bottom of the feeder mould, fill the mould with feed. Squeeze the method feeder into the mould, turn it over and press the underside of the mould to push the loaded feeder out. You should now have a neat pile of feed on the feeder with the hook and hook bait trapped inside. Some anglers like to add an extra layer of feed on top by half filling the mould and pressing the already loaded feeder a second time into the mould.

This can be handy if you are fishing in deep water as some of the feed will wash off on the way down, for the method to work well the hook and bait need to be in the feed.

Casting the feeder

Cast the loaded feeder using the same casting method described earlier, but with one minor change. Very gently feather the feeder down, but once it hits the water let it sink to the bottom unhindered. With the bail arm still open and the feeder on the bottom, move the rod round and place it in the rests. Now close the bail arm and reel in the slack line, as the line gets tighter it will begin to get pulled below the surface which is what we want. Continue winding line in until there is no slack left and the tip of the rod begins to get pulled round. Allow the tip to pull round an inch or two then stop winding. It is vital that the feeder does not move while the line is tightened, the feeder must stay exactly where it landed, any movement may cause the feeder to turn over or be pulled under debris on the bottom.

The neat simplicity of a loaded method feeder means they are ideal for casting against a feature like an island or weed bed. Casting to an island requires some accuracy in distance which is not always easy, fortunately there is an answer.

The line clip

Just about every fixed spool reel made now has a line clip, a simple device to govern the distance of each cast. Once set, you will be able to cast repeatedly to an island or reed bed and never end up casting too far and into trouble.

Lets imagine there is an island thirty yards in front of your swim, this is an obvious feature that you should investigate. Start with an empty feeder without the hook length attached, cast the feeder towards the island to land two or three feet from the bank. Feather the feeder down, but in the last second before it hits the water, lift your rod up to vertical and trap the line with your index finger against the lip of the spool as the feeder hits the water.

On the skirt of the spool there will be a button or knob, this is the line clip. While holding the line with your index finger, pass the line under the clip securing it in place, do not wind the line around the clip, just pass it under. Reel in as usual leaving the line under the clip and cast again.

On this cast feather down and lift the rod to vertical as the feeder approaches the water, but do not trap the line with your finger, this is where the line clip comes in. If you have cast too hard the line clip will stop the feeder in it's tracks and all the slack in the line will be taken up until the rod is reached. The rod will then bend and absorb the shock and the feeder will plop into the water. It's important that the rod is vertical at this point ready to absorb the shock of the feeder. If the rod was pointing down at the target, there would be nothing to absorb the shock and the line may break, not good.

Did your feeder land where you wanted?

Unclip the line and wind in or let out more line to correct the distance, clip up and cast again to check. Once you are happy with the distance, lay your rod down on the floor behind your seat, with the bail arm open walk along the bank with the feeder in your hand. When you feel the line reach the clip, place the feeder on the floor and mark it's location with a stick or whatever. Walk back to the rod and mark where the tip of the rod is. Now you have the exact distance marked out on the bank, it is an easy task to set the distance again if you should need to unclip for any reason. Some anglers like to have two bank sticks six feet apart and count how many turns around the sticks it takes to reach the clip. Others count the number of turns of the reel handle before the clip is reached, either way it's handy to know.

With the line clip in use, casting to an island or reed bed is much easier. Cast towards the feature raising the rod upright just before the feeder hits the water and feather the line.

Once you are sure the feeder has settled on the bottom, lay then rod in it's rests and tighten up to the feeder. Leave the line in the line clip for the next cast.

Bites on the feeder

A proper bite on a method feeder is unmistakable, because the feeder causes the fish to prick itself on the hook, as soon as the fish feels the hook it will bolt. As the fish bolts it will very quickly cause the soft tip of the rod to bend round, in fact if you are not paying attention your rod could be pulled into the water! Whenever a method feeder is fished, keep a very close eye on the rod or better still hold the rod butt in your lap.

Because the line is taught from the rod tip to the feeder, any fish bumping into the line between the feeder and the rod will cause a knock at the tip. When the fish are hungry and actively searching for food, line bites, little knocks and pulls can become constant, you must learn to ignore these. It's only when the rod is positively pulled round should you pick the rod up.

Playing fish

Once hooked the next step is to get the fish close enough to scoop it up in your landing net. Because of the strength of tackle used, bullying or hauling the fish in may not be possible depending on how big the fish is. Playing the fish is our only option and is a skill that is learnt at the expense of several lost fish.

Hold the rod with the reel foot between your ring finger and little finger, ensure you can reach the front edge of the spool with your index finger. The handle of the rod should rest against your forearm for support, but when a fish pulls hard use your other hand on the shaft of the rod to help take the strain. Where possible keep the rod at right angles to the line, it doesn't necessarily need to be upright, but keeping the rod at right angles will allow it to absorb any lunges by the fish.

Playing small fish

Granted, getting a 4oz Roach to the bank is not going to test your skills, but small fish have their own methods of escape. A 4oz Roach can wriggle and shake so quickly that they just throw the hook, which may not bother you too much, but it can unsettle the other fish in the area. Try to play and land every fish you hook, even the small ones.

Small fish are more likely to "bump" off the hook if the rod is too stiff, they somehow use the stiffness to bounce against the rod and cause the hook to come out. Because I recommended medium rods for your first rods, there is a good chance you will bounce the odd small Roach. Without buying a second lighter rod, I can only suggest you grip the rod lightly to allow more movement.

Small fish are also expert at unhooking themselves right at your feet, just as you either net them or swing them to hand. Again this is almost certainly due to the rod. Net small fish as soon as they are in reach of your landing net and don't give them the chance to bounce off.

Playing medium fish

Medium fish tend to be the easiest to land, they are too big to shake the hook out, but not powerful enough to control the fight. Their first run or two may cause the clutch to slip on the reel, but generally the runs are fairly short and run out of steam quickly.

Lets imagine you have hooked a 3lb Tench float fishing, with 4lb main line and a hook length of say 3lb. A Tench of 3lb is quite capable of breaking the line because of it's power. Tench have paddles as tails and can use them to produce surprisingly powerful runs pulling harder than the line strength. So long as the clutch is set loose enough the reel will let line out preventing a break. Once the fish has run a couple of times it will begin to tire, at this point they often wriggle and lunge in different directions seemingly with no plan in mind. These wriggles and lunges are not enough to cause the clutch to slip, instead the rod will bend and flex to absorb these lunges. Slowly reel the fish in coaxing it towards the bank, but don't think it's in the net yet. Tench in particular always seem to have energy in reserve and suddenly they will run again, but not necessarily towards open water. As they get closer to the bank fish often seem to remember a snag close to the bank they can bury themselves in. You need to react quickly, bring the rod tip down close to, or even under the water and pull the fish sideways causing it to swerve off course and hopefully out into open water.

The purpose of playing the fish is to tire it out until you have full control, then and only then reach for your landing net. By this time the fish should be on the surface too tired to dive down, draw the fish in with the rod and from under the water bring the net up around the fish, perfect.

Playing a large fish

This book is not about catching large fish we are more interested in just learning to fish, but one day a large fish will pick up your bait. Both float fishing and the method can attract a big fish often when least expected.

It can take a fish many years to grow big and in that time they would have been caught more than once. As soon as a big fish knows it's hooked it will head for the nearest snag, these fish know the lake very well and will take the shortest route as quickly as they can. Even with the feeder rod and it's 8lb line you will not stop a 20lb Carp when it runs, the only thing you can do is to try and steer it.

When a fish is running trying to stop it by simply holding the rod upright won't work, you will be pulling against the full power of the fish. Much better to steer it away from reed beds, tree roots and snags by pulling from the side. To steer a fish to the left, lower the tip close to or even under the water on your left, the line should now be coming from the fishes mouth and down it's left flank. The idea is to turn the fishes head, once the head turns the body will follow. A smart fish will know what you are doing straight away and will simply turn to the right slightly so you are once more pulling from behind. If this happens immediately switch the rod to your right side and continue the fishes right turn, but what if a right turn will take the fish to safety?

If you have no choice but to turn a fish either left or right and the fish is fighting back, your only choice is to increase the side pressure. Press your index finger against the front lip of the spool as it lets out line to artificially increase the drag and so increase the pull on the fish. This increase in pull will test your knots, hook length and main line to the limits which may result in a break. Fortunately you have Monofilament or Copolymer main line which is very forgiving, some high-tech lines have no give at all and will simply break.

If the fish is still on after one or two runs the fight should then be similar to a medium fish, keep in control until it is tired out and ready to net.

The fish made it to weeds

Most fish will magically take the hook from their mouths and impale it in the nearest reed, how they do this I don't know, but do it they do. In my experience Carp won't do this as quick as other fish, sometimes if you immediately stop pulling and leave the Carp a few minutes it will swim out of the reeds still hooked. Hold the line between your fingers and very gently pull on it to feel for the fish, when you feel the fish move out of the reeds, continue the fight.

If the hook is in a reed stem you will have no choice but to pull until either the hook pulls free or the hook length breaks. Don't pull with the rod, put the rod to one side and pull only on the main line. Be aware that the rig may come free with a start which can cause it to fly back at you, a feeder or hook in the face is very dangerous. Try not to pull the line in a straight line with your face or body, pull with your hands close to the ground and turn your head away.

Playing when using the line clip

One slight problem with using a line clip is if the fish runs and takes line it will reach the clip in no time. Some of the latest reels have line clips that release when playing a fish, but if yours doesn't you will have to quickly reach in and pull the line off the clip. Personally I don't use the line clip in open water, only when I cast against a feature like an island, that way the fish can only run to the side.

Unhooking the fish

Once netted the fish can be lifted out of the water, with larger fish lift by the frame of the net to avoid breaking the landing net handle. Smaller fish can be unhooked over the landing net in your lap, but larger fish should be placed on a unhooking mat on the ground, preferably on grass.

Method feeder fishing often produces fish hooked in the front of the mouth, the hook can be easily removed with the fingers. If the hook is out of reach then use the artery forceps to reach into the fishes mouth and grip the shaft of the hook to unhook the fish.

The small hooks used in float fishing can often be difficult to remove by hand even when at the front of the fishes mouth. Use a disgorger to reach and remove the hook. Whether you use the standard disgorger or a Slammo, place the slot in the disgorger over the hook length and follow the line down to the hook. Keeping the line tight on the disgorger, gently push against the hook to release it and then carefully draw it out of the fishes mouth with the disgorger.

With the fish unhooked take a moment to admire your catch and perhaps take a photo, but please return the fish as soon as possible. Use the landing net to take the fish from the unhooking mat to the water. Never stand up holding a fish, by their very nature fish are difficult to hold and dropping a fish will cause serious injury or fatal injury. When releasing a fish, support it carefully in the water until it is ready to swim. Never drop or throw fish back into the water.

Fishing on the surface

After catching fish on the bottom and catching fish mid water, there is one place left, the surface.

Chub, Rudd and Carp are the main species sought when surface fishing. Although Chub are a river species they are often found in lakes either by accident or by design, Rudd are common in still waters and can provide excellent sport on light gear. But on a hot summers day the fish that can be seen at the surface most often are the Carp, as anglers we just have to try to catch them.

Carp love the warm weather, on some waters they can be clearly see slowly, aimlessly, swimming around in the sunlight without a care in the world. On some busy venues though the Carp are less inclined to show themselves, I imagine the constant movement of anglers makes them uneasy.

So if you can, find a quiet water that you know to be stocked with Carp and spend an evening fishing "off the top".

The rod

A standard ledger rod with a through action is best suited to the task. The action of a rod is essentially the way the rod has been designed to bend under strain. With a through action rod the whole length of the rod down to the handle will bend when playing a fish. A rod like this is very forgiving and is capable of absorbing the most violent of lunges by fish.

Standard ledger rods are also graded by their power which is described by the test curve in pounds. The test curve is how much weight is required when hung on the line, to pull the rod tip down to an angle of 90 degrees to the handle held horizontal. For general purpose ledgering, and in this case fishing off the top, a test curve of one and a half pounds with 8lb main line is ideal.

A floating bait

To catch fish from the surface a floating bait is required, ready made baits can be bought from a tackle shop, but bread is still one of the best baits and is cheap and readily available. Thick sliced white bread or a fresh tin loaf are preferred. With sliced bread cut the slices into squares of an inch or more, with a tin loaf simply break chunks off for the hook.

Even with a hook inside, a lump of bread will

float more than long enough for the fish to find it. Trouble is so can ducks and small fish which will can become a real nuisance. If the lake has fowl then try to find an area away from them, small fish can only be defeated by using a tougher purpose made baits.

The rig

Floating baits are too light to cast on their own, a bubble float or controller float is added to the rig as a casting weight. I have to say I have never used a modern controller float, I prefer the simplicity of a bubble float.

A bubble float is a hollow plastic ball that can be filled with water. Filling the bubble two thirds with lake water, provides enough weight for casting and the remaining air trapped inside keeps the bubble afloat.

As usual the hook length should be weaker than the 8lb main line. You could use some of the 4lb line from your other spool, but I would recommend 6lb Monofilament line if you have it. The hook length needs to be three feet long, I don't remember ever seeing a ready made one, so we will tie our own.

Starting with the hook, use a size 8 or 10 that is silver in colour, I have found that black or brown hooks are often seen by the fish. The Kamasan Animal barbless eyed hook is a good example.

Tie the hook to three feet of 6lb line with a Uni knot and tie a figure of eight loop in the tail end.

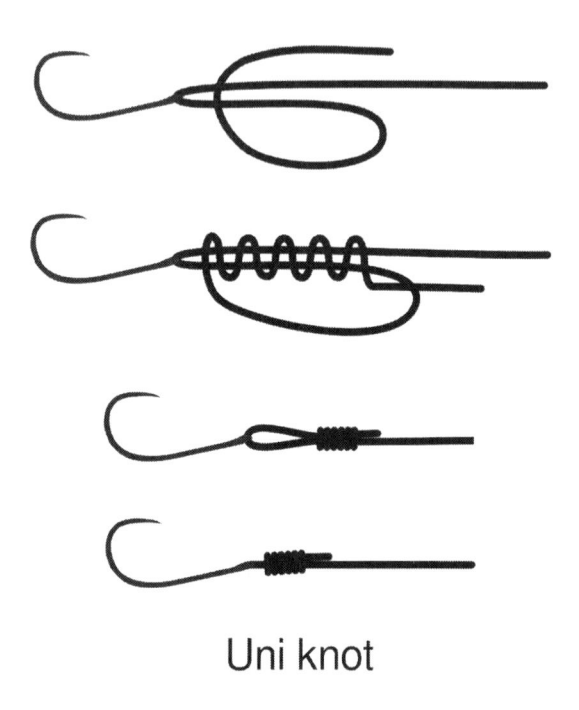

Uni knot

With the rod set up, pass the main line through the bushed holes in the flange around the bubble float, then tie a loop knot in the end. Attach the hook length through and through (loop to loop) and fix the bubble float in place above the loops with a small shot either side.

It's important that all of the rig floats including the line, coat the hook length and several feet of the main line with line floatant or Vaseline.

This will cause the line to stay on the surface. Any coils or loops of line hanging below the surface will be visible to the fish alerting them to the danger.

A patient approach

Fishing on the surface is a very exciting method because you can see the fish as they approach and take the bait. But it can also be very frustrating as the fish turn away at the last second or ignore your bait altogether.

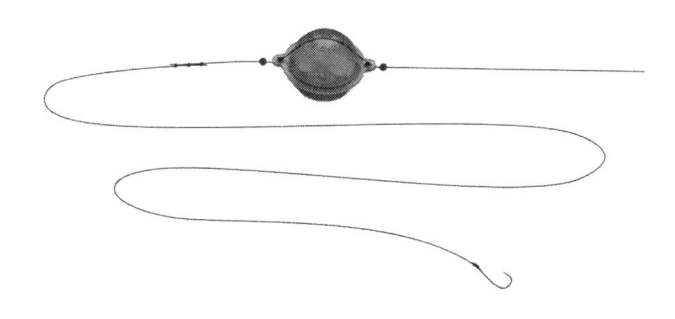

Bubble float rig

Fish are not mindless eating machines, they will only eat when they feel like it. So there will be times, especially in hot weather, when they will not be interested in food during the day. All you can do is wait until the evening, as the sun gets lower the fish will begin to feed.

Start by catapulting just two or three lumps of bread an inch or two in size out into the lake. If the bread is falling short, dip each piece briefly in the water to make it heavier. Now just wait and see if the fish will eat your free offerings. If they do then feed another couple of pieces, but try not to overfeed them. You should notice that the fish will take the free offerings with more confidence as time goes by, once you have the fish feeding, cast your bait.

Bury the hook in a piece of bread the same size as the free offerings, cast out and feather the line down. Allow the bait and bubble float to drift naturally, but if too much slack line develops then just gently pick the rod up and lift the slack line off the surface and reel in as you lower the rod down again.

Hooking the fish

Hold the rod all the time the rig is fishing, bites can be fast and unexpected. But when you can see a fish approaching your bait stay calm, wait just a second or two to ensure the fish has the bait in it's mouth before striking. On many occasions the fish will be pricked by the hook as the resistance of the bubble float comes into play, causing the fish to bolt. Play the fish as usual but expect a good fight, fish are cold blooded so when the water is warm they have bags of energy.

After catching a few you may have to move as the fish quickly realise what's going on. Use the same feed and catch routine in the new swim.

Stalking

Late in the day Carp often come in close to the bank to feed, especially on quiet waters. With the Carp at your feet, casting is not needed so free lining is the best approach.

Tie a hook directly to the end of the main line, no other tackle is needed, no float, no shot and no weaker hook length. This is one of the few occasions when a weaker hook length is not required. The hook knot will weaken the line slightly, so if there is a break it will almost certainly be at the knot leaving just the hook behind.

As we've been fishing off the top all day, why not continue in the margins. Stalk covertly along the bank with just your rod, bait, landing net, mat and artery forceps. Wearing polarized glasses the fish should be easy to spot, simply drop the bait onto the surface of the water near the fish and watch. If the fish are a few feet out, then quickly dip the bread on the hook in the water and swing it out underarm.

Being so close it should be easy to see when the fish takes the bait, strike and hold on tight. This is when a through action rod is essential, with the fish so close the first run will be powerful and instant. Without a through action rod to absorb the initial lunge, the line would almost certainly break.

If the fish are feeding on the bottom they will create clouds of mud in the water betraying their presence. On these occasions it may be better to offer a sunken piece of bread, with their heads down they can easily miss a floating bait.

Mount a piece of bread on the hook by squeezing half of it around the shank, ensure the point is exposed.

With half the bread compressed the bait will slowly sink to the bottom. To know when you have a bite, watch the line for movement or gently hold the line between your finger and feel for the fish.

Fish caught close in cause quite a commotion scaring any other fish away, it's unlikely you will catch more than one in the same place.

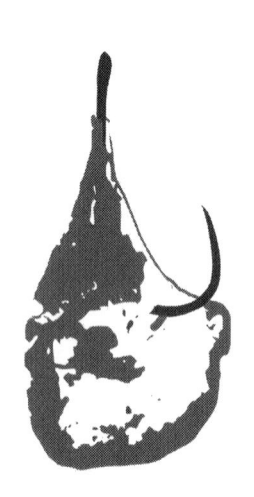

Stalking like this is a little opportunistic, but to make it a more planned method try pre-baiting. During the afternoon, walk along the bank and drop some feed in the margins at likely looking locations. Then later, visit each location to see if any fish are feeding. With luck you will be able to catch a fish at each spot.

What next ?

We have covered a few essential skills which will give you a good start. Spend a season just catching fish to practice your new skills. You may find there is an aspect of angling that you really enjoy or that you are particularly good at. Many anglers become specialists in one part of fishing, whereas others become good all rounders.

All I ask is that you enjoy your fishing and perhaps one day show someone else how it's done.

Handling the fish

Always use an unhooking mat spread on a soft flat surface.

Be aware of watch straps, lapel badges and jewellery that could catch on or damage fish.

Return fish to the water as quickly as possible, handle the fish as little as possible.

Covering the head of the fish will help keep it calm.

Deep-hooked fish should survive if the hook cannot be removed. Cut the line as far into the mouth as possible. Do not pull hard on the line and always release the fish immediately.

When releasing a fish, support it carefully in the water until it is ready to swim.

Never drop or throw fish back into the water.

When holding a fish, support it properly and keep it close to the ground, over an unhooking mat.

Never stand holding as fish, dropping it could be fatal for the fish.

Printed by Amazon Italia Logistica S.r.l.
Torrazza Piemonte (TO), Italy